Collaborating for Change

EDITED BY PEGGY HOLMAN AND TOM DEVANE

Open Space Technology

HARRISON OWEN
WITH GUEST APPEARANCE
BY ANNE STADLER

Copyright © 1999 by Harrison Owen and Anne Stadler

All rights reserved. No part of this publication may be reproduced, distributed, or transmitted in any form or by any means, including photocopying, recording, or other electronic or mechanical method, without the prior written permission of the publisher, except in the case of brief quotations embodied in critical reviews. For permissions requests, write to the publisher, addressed "Attention: Permissions Coordinator," at the address below:

Berrett-Koehler Communications, Inc.
450 Sansome Street, Suite 1200
San Francisco, CA 94111-3320

ORDERING INFORMATION

Please send orders to Berrett-Koehler Communications, P.O. Box 565, Williston, VT 05495. Or place your order by calling 800-929-2929, faxing 802-864-7626, or visiting www.bkconnection.com.
Special discounts are available on quantity purchases. For details, call 800-929-2929. See the back of this booklet for more information and an order form.

Printed in the United States of America on acid-free and recycled paper.

CONTENTS

Introduction   1
   Voices That Count: Realizing the Potential of Change
   Peggy Holman and Tom Devane

Open Space Technology   7
   Frequently Asked Questions   10
   Getting Started   14
   Roles, Responsibilities, and Relationships   14
   Impact on Power and Authority   16
   Conditions for Success   17
   Theoretical Basis   17
   Sustaining Results   18
   Final Comments   19

Notes   21

Resources   23
   Where to Go for More Information

Questions for Thinking Aloud   25

The Authors   27

INTRODUCTION

Voices That Count: Realizing the Potential of Change

Peggy Holman and Tom Devane

As seen through the lens of history, change is inevitable. Just look at any history book. Everything from fashions to attitudes has changed dramatically through the years. Change reflects underlying shifts in values and expectations of the times. Gutenberg's invention of the movable type printing press in the fifteenth century, for example, bolstered the developing humanism of the Renaissance. The new technology complemented the emerging emphasis on individual expression that brought new developments in music, art, and literature. Economic and political shifts paralleled the changing tastes in the arts, creating a prosperous and innovative age—a stark contrast to the preceding Middle Ages.

On the surface, technology enables greater freedom and prosperity. Yet this century has overwhelmed us with new technologies: automobiles, airplanes, radios, televisions, telephones, computers, the Internet. What distinguishes change today is the turbulence created by the breathtaking pace required to assimilate its effects.

In terms of social change, one trend is clear: People are demanding a greater voice in running their own lives. Demonstrated by the American Revolution and affirmed more recently in the fall of the Berlin Wall, the riots in Tiananmen Square, the social unrest in Indonesia, and the redistribution of power in South Africa, this dramatic shift in values and expectations creates enormous potential for positive change today.

So, why does change have such a bad reputation?

One reason is that change introduces uncertainty. While change holds the possibility of good things happening, 80 percent of us see only its negative aspects.[1] And even when people acknowledge their current situation is far from perfect, given the choice between the devil they know or the devil they don't, most opt for the former. The remedy we are learning is to involve people in creating a picture of a better future. Most of us are drawn toward the excitement and possibility of change and move past our fear of the unknown.

Another reason we are wary of change is that it can create winners and losers. Clearly the British were not happy campers at the end of the American Revolution. In corporations, similar battle lines are often drawn between those with something to lose and those with something to gain. The real challenge is to view the change *systemically* and ask what's best for both parties in the post-change environment.

Finally, many people have real data that change is bad for them. These change survivors know that "flavor of the month" change initiatives generally fall disappointingly short. In our organizations and communities, many people have experienced the results of botched attempts at transformational change. Like the cat that jumps on a hot stove only once, it's simple human nature to avoid situations that cause pain. And let's face it, enough change efforts have failed to create plenty of cynicism over the past ten years. For these people, something had better "smell" completely different if they're going to allow themselves to care.

Ironically, as demands for greater involvement in our organizations increased, leaders of many well-publicized, large-scale change efforts moved the other way and totally ignored people. They chose instead to focus on more visible and seemingly easier-to-manage components such as information technology, strategic architectures, and business processes. Indeed, "Downsize" was a ubiquitous battle cry of the nineties. According to a 1996 *New York Times* poll, "Nearly three-quarters of all households have had a close encounter with layoffs since 1980. In one-third of all households, a family member has lost a job, and nearly 40 percent more know a relative, friend, or neighbor who was laid off."[2] The individual impact has been apparent in the increased stress, longer working hours, and reduced sense of job security chronicled in virtually every recent book and article on change.

To paraphrase Winston Churchill, "Never before in the field of human endeavors was so much screwed up by so few for so many." By ignoring the need to involve people in something that affects them, many of today's popular change methods have left a bad taste in the mouths of "change targets" (as one popular methodology calls those affected) for *any* type of change. They have also often left behind less effective organizations with fewer people and lower morale. Consequently, even well-intentioned, well-designed change efforts have a hard time getting off the ground.

If an organization or community's leaders *do* recognize that emerging values and rapidly shifting environmental demands call for directly engaging people in change, they often face another challenge. When the fear of uncertainty, the potential for winners and losers, and the history of failures define change, how can they systematically involve people and have some confidence that it will work? That is where this booklet comes in.

A Way Through

This booklet offers an approach that works because it acknowledges the prevailing attitudes toward change. It offers a fresh view based on the possibility of a more desirable future, experience with the whole system, and activities that signal "something different is happening this time." That difference systematically taps the potential of human beings to make themselves, their organizations, and their communities more adaptive and more effective. This approach is based on solid, proven principles for unleashing people's creativity, knowledge, and spirit toward a common purpose.

How can this be? It does so by filling two huge voids that most large-scale change efforts miss. The first improvement is *intelligently involving people* in changing their workplaces and communities. We have learned that creating a collective sense of purpose, sharing information traditionally known only to a few, valuing what people have to contribute, and inviting them to participate in meaningful ways positively affects outcomes. In other words, informed, engaged people can produce dramatic results.

The second improvement is a *systemic* approach to change. By asking "Who's affected? Who has a stake in this?" we begin to recognize that no change happens in isolation. Making the interdependencies explicit enables shifts based on a common view of the whole. We can each play our part while understanding our contribution to the system. We begin to understand that in a change effort the "one-party-wins-and-one-party-loses" perception need not necessarily be the case. When viewed from a systemic perspective, the lines between "winners" and "losers" become meaningless as everyone participates in cocreating the future for the betterment of all. The advantages are enormous: coordinated actions and closer relationships lead to simpler, more effective solutions.

The growing numbers of success stories are beginning to attract attention. Hundreds of examples around the world of dramatic and sustained increases in organization and community performance now exist.[3] With such great potential, why isn't everyone operating this way? The catch with high-involvement, systemic change is that more people have their say. Until traditional managers are ready to say yes to that, no matter how stunning the achievements of others, these approaches will remain out of reach for most and a competitive advantage for a few.

Our Purpose

This booklet describes an approach that has helped others achieve dramatic, sustainable results in their organization or communities. Our purpose is to provide basic information that you can use to decide whether this approach is right for you. We give you an overview including an illustrative story, answers to frequently asked questions and tips for getting started. We've also given you discussion questions for "thinking aloud" with others and a variety of references to learn more.

There is ample evidence that when high involvement and a system-wide approach are used, the potential for unimagined results is within reach. As Goethe so eloquently reminds us, "Whatever you can do or dream you can, begin it. Boldness has genius, power, and magic in it."

What are you waiting for?

Open Space Technology

The times, they are a-changin'.
—Bob Dylan

AT&T had an interesting problem. The design team it had assembled to create its pavilion for the 1996 Olympics had lived up to all expectations. The design, in fact, was so good that AT&T was invited to move its pavilion from the edge of the Olympic Village to dead center. Since exposure was the name of the game, and $200 million was riding on the project, making the move was an easy decision. There was, however, one small problem. At the edge of the Global Village, 5,000 visitors per day could be expected. At the center that number moved up dramatically: 75,000 people at the gate. Talk about exposure—but clearly a structure designed for 5,000 would not accommodate 75,000. To make matters worse, the original design had taken ten months to complete, and it was now December with the Olympics a bare six months away.

The 23 members of the design team were a dispirited group when they assembled to meet the challenge. They knew they were good, and given the time they could easily rise to the occasion. But the time was not there. As they sat in a circle, preparing to engage in what they perceived to be a very doubtful enterprise called Open Space Technology, one of their number was heard to comment, "I think we are about ready to turn a disaster into a catastrophe."

Two days later, the atmosphere was rather different. A totally new design had been created down to the level of working drawings, and everybody agreed that aesthetically it was much better than the earlier one. In terms of implementation, they were actually further along with the new design than they had been with the old one, for as they planned they were also ordering materials for delivery. Perhaps most important, everybody was still talking to each other, and some even described the undertaking as "fun," complaining only that they should have used Open Space the first time.

Here is a systemwide, long-term Open Space story from Anne Stadler, an Open Space practitioner of many years:

> In May 1996, 120 faculty, students, and staff from all Fred Hutchinson Cancer Research Center (FHCRC) divisions attended an unusual two-day retreat. Focusing on the theme "Integrating basic, clinical, and epidemiological sciences to understand human biology and disease," they used Open Space Technology to initiate conversations and generate practical activities.
>
> It took foresight and courage to bring this about. The FHCRC, 2,000 people strong, was organized by traditional scientific disciplines. It is a global leader in cancer research. So why tamper with success?
>
> Dr. Lee Hartwell, a highly respected geneticist, initiated the effort. He believed that only through synthesizing basic, clinical, and population sciences would we understand fundamentals of human biology and disease. The crucial answers would no longer come from isolated pursuits of different disciplines. Hartwell chose Open Space Technology to support maximum opportunity for self-organizing. He felt this would reveal the nascent leadership for collaboration, learning, and action. The choice had his colleagues scratch-

ing their heads. People asked, "Who are the speakers? What is the agenda?" When told they would create the agenda on the spot, most colleagues were skeptical. However, once people were confronted with an open agenda and invited to take responsibility for what they cared about, leaders emerged to convene conversations.

That first meeting generated several cross-disciplinary initiatives, including a monthly graduate and postgraduate seminar, internal Web pages for each laboratory, a dual-mentored training program, and several interdisciplinary courses, minicourses, workshops, and lectures. The event unleashed new leadership and enthusiastic participation.

In 1997, Dr. Hartwell was named FHCRC president/director. His first act: convening another centerwide Open Space event. This created new relationships and projects, including a long-term, four-division interdisciplinary research program, more courses, some reorganization, and ongoing work on diversity and leadership development. Reflecting on the FHCRC's year-old Open Space era, Hartwell said, "I have found that leadership in daily actions and issues is key. To effect significant change, many people must become leaders."

FHCRC's current challenge is becoming a continuous Open Space learning community, fostering efficient communication among multiple sites with different cultures. Kim Wells, organization development director, keeps the space open for the evolving learning community. She reports: "I've been offering classes in leadership of complex systems; we've started regular two-hour Open Space learning exchanges, and we are considering an Open Space on diversity within the year. Using our intranet for communication and tracking what people are doing and learning is a future prospect."

Based on the Fred Hutchinson Cancer Research Center's two years of experience, opening space in an organization has these cycles:

- convening the circle (calling all relevant stakeholders together on a timely and relevant subject),
- revealing the leadership and diversity present (through self-organizing a marketplace),
- manifesting practical outcomes in day-to-day work,
- supporting the leadership in oneself and others to respond to emergent realities and possibilities,
- sharing learning through reflection and storytelling.

Frequently Asked Questions

What Is It?

At the very least, Open Space is a fast, cheap, and simple way to better, more productive meetings. At a deeper level, it enables people to experience a very different quality of organization in which self-managed work groups are the norm, leadership is a constantly shared phenomenon, diversity becomes a resource to be used instead of a problem to be overcome, and personal empowerment is a shared experience. It is also fun. In a word, the conditions are set for fundamental organizational change; indeed, that change may already have occurred. By the end, groups face an interesting choice. They can do it again, they can do it better, or they can go back to their prior mode of behavior.

When Is It Used?

Open Space is appropriate in situations where a major issue must be resolved, characterized by high levels of complexity, high levels of diversity (in terms of the people involved), the presence of potential or actual conflict, and with a decision time of yesterday.

What Are the Probable Outcomes?

Depending on the length of time involved (one to three days), the following are essentially guaranteed: Every issue of concern to anybody in the group will be on the table. All issues will have been discussed to the extent that the interested parties choose to do so. A full record of the proceedings from the discussions will be in the hands of the participants upon departure. Priorities will have been identified, related issues converged, and initial action steps identified. And the people in the organization will have experienced a very different and self-empowering way of working that they can take back with them. Substantive outcomes have ranged from organization redesign to strategic plan development to product design, to name a few.

How Does It Work?

Open Space runs on two fundamentals: passion and responsibility. Passion engages the people in the room. Responsibility ensures that tasks get done. A focusing theme or question provides the framework for the event. The art of framing the question lies in saying just enough to evoke attention, while leaving sufficient open space for the imagination to run wild.

All participants are seated in a circle (or concentric circles if the group is large). I have found that the circle is the fundamental geometry of open human communication; have you ever heard of a *square* of friends? The four principles and the one law that guide life in Open Space are introduced. The participants are invited to identify any issue for which they have some genuine passion and are prepared to take personal responsibility. With the issue(s) in mind they come to the center of the circle, write their issue on a piece of paper, announce it to the group, and post the paper on the wall. When all the issues that anybody cares to identify have surfaced, the group is invited to go to the wall, sign up for the issues they care to deal with, and get to work. No matter what the group size, all this takes somewhat more than an hour. From that point on, the group is self-managing. As the groups meet, reports of their activities are generated (typically on computers), and at the conclusion (in a three-day event) all issues are prioritized. The "hot" issues are developed in further detail with concrete action as the goal.

The Principles of Open Space

Whoever comes is the right people. This reminds people that it is not how many people or the position they hold that counts, rather it is their passion for the subject that is important. So what happens if nobody comes to your group? Well, when was the last time you had the time to work on an idea you really cared about? Even a group of one works.

Whatever happens is the only thing that could have happened. This is a reminder to let go of what might have been, should have been, or could have been. It is in moments of surprise, large and small, that real learning and growth occur.

When it starts is the right time. Creativity and spirit don't happen according to the clock; they appear in their own time. Open Space merely reminds us that clocks are human-made constructs and have very little to do with the right time for things.

When it's over, it's over. This offers a marvelous way to save time and aggravation. If you get together and it takes ten minutes to do what you wanted, congratulations! Move on and do something else. If, on the other hand, you find yourself deeply engaged in what you are doing, keep doing it until you are finished.

These principles are simple statements of the way the world works. While they may appear counterintuitive to some, they are my observations of what always happens when people interact.

The Law of Two Feet (sometimes called the Law of Personal Initiative) says to stand up for what you believe, and if you feel you are neither contributing nor learning where you are, use your two feet and go somewhere else. The law is fundamentally about personal responsibility. It makes it clear that the only person responsible for your experience is you.

The actual Open Space event lasts from one to three days, depending on desired outcomes. One day allows for the raising and discussion of pertinent issues. In two days a useful set of proceedings can be generated. With an additional half day, all issues may be prioritized, converged, and brought to a point of action. Shorter times are possible but with a genuine loss of depth.

Life After Open Space

To the best of my knowledge, no organization comes away unaffected by Open Space. In addition to whatever substantive outcomes may have emerged from the gathering, the subtle effects may have even more impact. At the very least, the organization has a new performance benchmark, for all participants now know that endless preparation is not required for useful engagement. Distributed leadership, personal empowerment, appreciation of diversity, even self-managed work groups are all a matter of experience. Of course the group may choose never to experience this again, but there is no denying that all of the above took place.

Cost Justification

Since there is virtually no up-front planning or training required (except for theme identification and logistics) and only one facilitator necessary regardless of the group size, costs can range from essentially nothing to whatever the group is prepared to spend for accommodations, travel, and the like. Run these costs against the benefit of doing in two days what had previously taken ten months on a $200 million project, and the justification is pretty clear. Needless to say, not every instance of Open Space produces those sorts of results, but they are not uncommon.

Getting Started

When contemplating fundamental change, my first advice is "If it ain't broke, don't fix it." In short, make sure you really want to take this trip before you start. With specific reference to Open Space, the advice is "If you can find any other way to do what you want to do, do it." The reason is simple. With Open Space, the good news and the bad news are identical: it works. In Open Space, every group I have worked with becomes excited, innovative, creative, and ready to assume responsibility for what the members care about. This all sounds wonderful, but for some people sometimes, it also sounds like a prescription for going out of control. And they are right. If maintaining control is your fundamental intent, for goodness' sake don't even think about Open Space. On the other hand, if you are prepared to believe in people, trust them, and acknowledge that in all probability they are the true experts about what needs to be done, then Open Space will deliver. And you can be sure that fundamental change is a likely consequence.

Roles, Responsibilities, and Relationships

Sponsorship Requirements

The sponsors must be prepared to honor and respect all the participants. This does not mean that every crazy idea generated in the course of the gathering must be implemented, and there will be some crazy ideas. But it does mean that the space created must be safe for people to be fully creative and fully themselves. As a matter of fact, groups I have worked with are rather conservative, whether they be corporations, communities, religious orders, or major political jurisdictions, and collectively they prove to be excellent judges regarding the insanity or applicability of an idea.

Role of the Facilitator

The job of the facilitator is to create a safe space in which people can work and then to get out of the way. Observably, the facilitator has a

OPEN SPACE TECHNOLOGY 15

	Before	During	After
Sponsor(s)/ Convenor(s)	• Express the need • Commit to letting go of control • Commit the resources • Identify whom to invite	• Be fully present	• Support the outcomes • Stay open to where the experience takes the organization
Designer/ Facilitator	• Support the convenors in expressing the theme • Do due diligence in making the sponsor aware that once the organization has been "opened," it doesn't go back	• Create a safe place	• Coach the sponsor(s) on staying open to what emerges from the organization—sometimes it can be unfamiliar and uncomfortable
Participants		• Be fully present	• Follow through on commitments • Bring the four principles and the law back with you

Table 1. Roles and Responsibilities

maximum of 20 minutes "up front" and from that point on apparently does nothing. He or she will not intervene in any of the groups, or with the group as a whole, unless a Space Invader presents himself or herself. Space Invaders may be just overly enthusiastic participants or (in the worst case) the chairman of the board, who is concerned that things are out of control. Space Invaders take it upon themselves to corral everybody into a single course of action of their design. Open Space is the quintessential "trust the group—trust the process" sort of thing, and *nobody* has the right to control specific outcomes, so long as he or she chooses to be in Open Space.

Participants' Role

The simple answer to who participates in Open Space is whoever cares. In practice, the invitation goes to everyone who might care about the answers to the theme or framing question, whether from within the organization or from outside. Where the logistics are a challenge, there are a variety of ways to handle the situation, such as limiting attendance to first come, first served, or to a certain number from each community affected.

The job of the participants is to be fully themselves. If they are scared, trustless, frustrated, so be it. And if they are enthusiastic, creative, and ready for innovation, that is good, too. They are the way they are, and that is precisely the way they should be. Expectations of the participants (and that means everybody, including the planning committee, executive staff, and chairman of the board) are that they will come, be fully present, and be open to outcomes—and then take personal responsibility for ensuring that good and useful activities occur. All of this is not the sort of thing that a rousing speech on values and responsibilities is likely to engender. But it seems to take place, almost as a matter of course, in situations where genuine respect is present.

For those who are not able to participate, the proceedings and the people who were there provide the connection to the experience. What happens after that is guided by the passion and responsibility of those who participated and what they bring back with them.

A Word on Planning Committees

Open Space presents a problem to planning committees. There is very little to be done in advance. As a matter of fact, my major effort with such committees is to help them understand that after the theme has been determined and the guests have been invited, all the rest is quite simple and straightforward logistics. Rent the hall, arrange for meals, and let it happen. Self-organization does have its advantages.

Impact on Power and Authority

Open Space can be very problematical for positional power and authority, particularly if those who hold that power and authority are in any substantial way insecure. For "control freaks," Open Space is an anathema and should never be used. However, when power and authority are rooted in competence, respect, accountability, and trust, Open Space becomes a very natural way of doing business. There was a time, not long ago, when executives at all levels were expected to be in control and know all the answers. I suspect that time has passed. For those in executive positions who share my suspicion, Open Space can be a very useful method to use.

Conditions for Success

When to Use It: Use Open Space whenever the answer is basically unknown and the only possible hope is that the group members, consisting of all those who care, can from their collective wisdom arrive at solutions that no individual or small group can hope to devise.

Why It Works: Open Space is an evolving mystery. By all rights it should not work. But it does. The answers to the question of why it works will come from what we know, and are finding out, about self-organizing systems.

When Not to Use This Method: Do not use this method if you wish to remain in total control, at least as we used to understand *total* and *control*. Control and accountability are still very much present in Open Space, but the locus of both shifts from one, wise, all-powerful executive to the participants themselves.

Common Mistakes: Open Space is remarkably forgiving. Indeed, the only way I know to totally undermine the process is to think that you are in charge of it (see above).

Theoretical Basis

Open Space Technology was not the product of careful design. It occurred simply because I was tired of organizing meetings only to discover that the best-loved part was the coffee breaks, the only part I had nothing to do with. The immediate inspiration was social organization in tribal West Africa, where I discovered that everything of importance and utility occurred in a circle. Every indigenous population of which I am aware made the same discovery a long time before I did.

Retrospectively, as we try to figure out why Open Space works, the answers generally come from research dealing with self-organization, complex adaptive systems, "dissipative structures," and the like. The associated names are not generally found in the literature of management or even behavioral science and include the likes of Stuart Kaufmann (biologist), Ilya Prigogine (chemist), and Murray Gel-Mann (physicist), to name a few. At the level of popularization we should also include Meg Wheatley and her work presented under the titles *Leadership and the New Science* and, more recently, *A Simpler Way*.

Sustaining Results

So you had a great gathering. What do you do next? The answer is quite simple but perhaps not totally satisfactory: Go with the flow. Concretely, this means that in an Open Space gathering the emergent structure, purpose, and power of an organization will not only reveal themselves but will be mapped out in terms of the proceedings and what follows. The smart money will support the energy. Where it is strong (coherent and useful) it will provide resources and break down barriers (as in bureaucratic constraints), and where it is weak, don't proceed.

The choice of an immediate next step is usually pretty clear and typically is one of three possibilities:

- the actions to be taken are so clear it only remains to do them;
- the actions to be taken are pretty clear, but more information or consultation is required, in which case it is important to set a time by which these tasks will be completed;
- the issue remains clear as mud, in which case a reasonable next step would be to hold another Open Space event, this time devoted exclusively to that issue.

There is also a major opportunity to anchor the new organizational behaviors experienced in Open Space. As mentioned, self-managed work groups, distributed leadership, appreciation of diversity, and self-empowerment, among others, appear as natural by-products of the Open Space environment. Typically, however, these behaviors manifest so quickly and easily that many of the participants will have missed their arrival. For an intact work group it is very useful to reflect upon the new arrivals. Such reflection should not be confused with standard training programs that previously had sought to engender these behaviors. When a group is already functioning as a self-managed work group (for example) it makes little sense to go back to the beginning with fundamental concepts and practices. In this case we are dealing with a matter of experience that may be acknowledged and built upon.

Final Comments

A number of people, when they first hear about Open Space, come away with the opinion that there is no structure and less control. This opinion is totally wrong. What is true is that there is no *preimposed* structure and control. Such structure and control as is present (and it turns out to be a lot) is all emergent from the people involved, the tasks they perform, and the environment in which they are operating. In short, it is *appropriate* structure and control—appropriate to the people, task, and environment.

In most cases, people who view Open Space as being out of control with no structure have not actually been in Open Space. Had they been there, they would know what 500 representatives knew after they had gathered to rethink the Presbyterian Church (U.S.A.). In the process the Presbyterians created 164 task groups, which were self-managed over a 48-hour period, ending with a book of proceedings (350 pages long) in their hands. All of this was not done by levitation. In short, the level of emergent structure and control is generally of a sort that no planning committee would dare imagine, let alone seek to implement. But it happens and it works. Such is the nature of self-organizing systems.

There also seems to be a notion that Open Space is good only for establishing useful conversation, with substantive contribution not a goal of the method. One author even described it as having the sole use as a forum for airing employee grievances. Doubtless, good conversations do take place; and grievances get aired—but substantive output, as in the case of AT&T, is no stranger.

Notes

[1] Oakley, Ed, and Doug Krug. *Enlightened Leadership.* Denver, Colo.: Stone Tree Publishing, 1991, p. 38.

[2] The *New York Times, The Downsizing of America.* New York: Times Books, 1996.

[3] Holman, Peggy, and Tom Devane, eds. *The Change Handbook: Group Methods for Shaping the Future.* San Francisco: Berrett-Koehler Publishers, 1999. This book contains over twenty such stories of stellar results from high-involvement, systemic change.

RESOURCES

Where to Go for More Information

Since our focus has been to give you an *introduction* to Open Space Technology, we want you to know where to go for more information. Here are books, articles, Web sites, and other sources that can help you develop a more in-depth understanding.

Organizations

H. H. Owen and Company
7808 River Falls Drive
Potomac, MD 20854
(301) 469-9269
(301) 983-9314 (fax)
owen@tmn.com (e-mail)
www.tmn.com/~owen (Web site)

Open Space Institute
(Currently in Australia, Canada, Germany, United States)
osi@tmn.com (e-mail)
www.tmn.com/openspace (Web site)
- Publications
- Stories
- Tips and tools
- Training and support

Open Space Technology References

Owen, Harrison. *Riding the Tiger*. Potomac, Md.: Abbott Publishing, 1991.

———. *The Millennium Organization*. Potomac, Md.: Abbott Publishing, 1994.

———. *Expanding Our Now: The Story of Open Space Technology*. San Francisco: Berrett-Koehler, 1997.

———. *Open Space Technology: A User's Guide*. (2nd ed.) San Francisco: Berrett-Koehler, 1997.

———. *The Spirit of Leadership: Liberating the Leader in Each of Us*. San Francisco: Berrett-Koehler, 1999.

———, ed. *Tales from Open Space*. Potomac, Md.: Abbott Publishing, 1995.

Stadler, Anne, guest ed. "Open Space." *At Work: Stories of Tomorrow's Workplace* (special issue) Vol. 6, No. 2 (March/April 1997).

Videos

Holman, Peggy (producer), Justin Harris (director). *U S WEST Open Space*. 1995. 16 minutes. An Open Space with 175 people in a work setting. Available through the Open Space Institute.

Stadler, Anne (producer). *Learning in Open Space*. 1991. 30 minutes. Available through Abbot Publishing.

Questions for Thinking Aloud

To gain additional value from this booklet, consider discussing it with others. Here are some questions you might find useful as you explore Open Space Technology and its application to your situation.

1. What attracted you to reading about Open Space? What situation(s) did you have in mind as possible applications? What fascinated you about what you read? What memories or experiences were triggered when you read this?

2. The Law of Two Feet calls on people to take responsibility for their passions. What difference do you think that would make?

3. Without being in Open Space, we have all experienced the four principles at some time. (Whoever comes is the right people. Whatever happens is the only thing that could have. When it starts is the right time. When it's over, it's over.) Describe an experience where you found value in following any of the Open Space principles.

4. A key element of Open Space is that people gather in a circle at the beginning and end of the day. When you have met in a circle, what did you notice about its impact on the quality of your interaction?

5. How do you imagine Open Space would affect current views of responsibility, authority, and control in your organization or community?

6. What need in your organization or community could be served through Open Space? What in your organization or community is calling this forth? Were you to proceed, who else do you want to be part of the conversation?

7. We all have hopes for what we want to achieve in our organizations and communities. How might Open Space Technology serve those hopes? What concerns would you have in using Open Space?

8. What's next?

The Authors

Harrison Owen is president of H. H. Owen and Company. His academic background and training centered on the nature and function of myth, ritual, and culture. In the middle 1960s, he left academe to work with a variety of organizations including small West African villages, urban (American and African) community organizations, the Peace Corps, Regional Medical Programs, The National Institutes of Health, and the Veterans Administration. Along the way he discovered that his study of myth, ritual, and culture had direct application to these social systems. In 1977 he created H. H. Owen and Company in order to explore the culture of organizations in transformation as a theorist and practicing consultant. Harrison convened the First International Symposium on Organization Transformation and is the originator of Open Space Technology. He is the author of *Spirit: Transformation and Development in Organizations, Leadership Is, Riding the Tiger, Open Space Technology: A User's Guide* (second edition, Berrett-Koehler), *The Millennium Organization, Tales from Open Space* (editor), and *Expanding Our Now: The Story of Open Space Technology.*

When once asked what he did, Harrison responded that he honestly didn't know, but his intent was to make human life human. He has worked in a variety of areas, from the African jungle to the halls of Congress—with large corporations in between. He believes that he has always been doing the same thing, and as he said above, Open Space seems to be more of the same.

Anne Stadler is a former television producer and community organizer who now opens space in organizations for the evolution of self-organizing learning communities. She is consulting faculty for the Antioch/Seattle Graduate Management Progams. Her consulting practice includes work in India and the United States with organizations as diverse as scientific research centers, schools, community arts centers, and businesses. She produced the video *Learning in Open Space*, in which Harrison Owen explains the philosophy and use of Open Space Technology.

Series Editors
Peggy Holman is a writer and consultant who helps organizations achieve cultural transformation. High involvement and a whole-systems perspective characterize her work. Her clients include AT&T Wireless Services, Weyerhaeuser Company, St. Joseph's Medical Center, and the U.S. Department of Labor. Peggy can be reached at (425) 746-6274 or pholman@msn.com.

Tom Devane is an internationally known consultant and speaker specializing in transformation. He helps companies plan and implement transformations that utilize highly participative methods to achieve sustainable change. His clients include Microsoft, Hewlett-Packard, AT&T, Johnson & Johnson, and the Republic of South Africa. Tom can be reached at (303) 898-6172 or tdevane@iex.net.

The Change Handbook

Group Methods for Shaping the Future

Edited by Peggy Holman and Tom Devane

The Change Handbook presents eighteen proven, highly successful change methods that enable organizations and communities of all shapes and sizes to engage and focus the energy and commitment of all their members These diverse participative change approaches, described in detail by their creators and expert practitioners, illustrate how organizations and communities today can achieve and sustain extraordinary results and foster a capacity to handle the inevitable turbulence along the way. By first systematically involving all organizational stakeholders in the change process, and then planning and implementing change simultaneously—in real time—these methods uniquely enable all members to become change agents, active participants in determining their organization's direction and future.

Marvin Weisbord, Merrelyn Emery, Masaaki Imai, Kathie Dannemiller, Harrison Owen, and many other leading thinkers and practitioners of organizational change show how to harness the vision, energy, and enthusiasm of the entire organization—from employees at all levels to key stakeholders to entire communities. In *The Change Handbook* they provide practical answers to frequently asked questions to that you can choose the methods that will work best in your participative change efforts.

> "In a world where change is the norm, where the effectiveness of organizations is a competitive advantage, and where we have more change methodologies available than most people could absorb in a lifetime, this book has identified how to match the best approach to the situation. While providing structured guidelines for organizational improvement, the authors acknowledge and celebrate the power of creativity and engaged people to provide the energy needed for successful change."
>
> —SUSAN MERSEREAU, *Vice President,*
> *Organizational Effectiveness, Weyerhaeuser Company*

Paperback original, approx. 450 pages, ISBN 1-57675-058-2
Item no. 50582-605   U.S. $49.95
To order call 800-929-2929 or visit www.bkconnection.com

Collaborating for Change
Peggy Holman and Tom Devane, Editors

The Collaborating for Change booklet series offers concise, comprehensive overviews of 14 leading change strategies in a convenient, inexpensive format. Adapted from chapters in *The Change Handbook*, each booklet is written by the originator of the change strategy or an expert practitioner, and includes

- An example of the strategy in action
- Tips for getting started
- An outline of roles, responsibilities, and relationships
- Conditions for success
- Keys to sustaining results
- Thought-provoking questions for discussion

If you're deciding on a change strategy for your organization and you need a short, focused treatment of several alternatives to distribute to your colleagues, or you've decided on a change strategy and want to disseminate information about it to get everyone on board, the Collaborating for Change booklets are the ideal choice.

♦ SEARCH CONFERENCE
Merrelyn Emery and Tom Devane
Uses open systems principles in strategic planning, thereby creating a well-articulated, achievable future with identifiable goals, a timetable, and action plans for realizing that future.

♦ FUTURE SEARCH
Marvin R. Weisbord and Sandra Janoff
Helps members of an organization or community discover common ground and create self-managed plans to move toward their desired future.

♦ THE CONFERENCE MODEL
Emily M. Axelrod and Richard H. Axelrod
Engages the critical mass needed for success in redesigning organizations and processes, co-creating a vision of the future, improving customer and supplier relationships, or achieving strategic alignment.

♦ THE WHOLE SYSTEMS APPROACH
Cindy Adams and W. A. (Bill) Adams
Creates a world of work where people and organizations thrive and produce outrageous individual and organizational results.

♦ PREFERRED FUTURING
Lawrence L. Lippitt
Mobilizes everyone involved in a human system to envision the future they want and then develop strategies to get there.

♦ THE STRATEGIC FORUM
Chris Soderquist
Answers "Can our strategy achieve our objectives?" by building shared understanding (a mental map) of how the organization or community really works.

♦ PARTICIPATIVE DESIGN WORKSHOP
Merrelyn Emery and Tom Devane
Enables an organization to function in an interrelated structure of self-managing work groups.

♦ GEMBA KAIZEN
Masaaki Imai and Brian Heymans
Builds a culture able to initiate and sustain change by providing skills to improve process, enabling employees to make daily improvements, installing JIT systems and lean process methods in administrative systems, and improving equipment reliability and product quality.

♦ THE ORGANIZATION WORKSHOP
Barry Oshry and Tom Devane
Develops the knowledge and skills of "system sight" that enable us to create partnerships up, down, and across organizational lines.

♦ WHOLE-SCALE CHANGE
Kathleen D. Dannemiller, Sylvia L. James, and Paul D. Tolchinsky
Helps organizations remain successful through fast, deep, and sustainable total system change by bringing members together as one-brain (all seeing the same things) and one-heart (all committed to achieving the same preferred future).

♦ OPEN SPACE TECHNOLOGY
Harrison Owen (with Anne Stadler)
Enables high levels of group interaction and productivity to provide a basis for enhanced organizational function over time.

♦ APPRECIATIVE INQUIRY
David L. Cooperrider and Diana Whitney
Supports full-voiced appreciative participation in order to tap an organization's positive change core and inspire collaborative action that serves the whole system.

♦ THINK LIKE A GENIUS PROCESS
Todd Siler
Helps individuals and organizations go beyond narrow, compartmentalized thinking; improve communication, teamwork, and collaboration; and achieve breakthrough thinking.

♦ REAL TIME STRATEGIC CHANGE
Robert W. Jacobs and Frank McKeown
Uses large, interactive group meetings to rapidly create an organization's preferred future and then sustain it over time.

Collaborating for Change Order Form
Each booklet comes shrinkwrapped in packets of 6

Order in Quantity and Save!
1–4 packets: $45 per packet • 5–9 packets: $40.50 per packet
10–49 packets: $38.25 per packet • 50–99 packets: $36 per packet

# of Packets		Item #	Price
_____	Search Conference	6058X-605	_____
_____	Future Search	60598-605	_____
_____	The Strategic Forum	60601-605	_____
_____	Participative Design Workshop	6061X-605	_____
_____	Gemba Kaizen	60628-605	_____
_____	The Whole Systems Approach	60636-605	_____
_____	Preferred Futuring	60644-605	_____
_____	The Organization Workshop	60652-605	_____
_____	Whole-Scale Change	60660-605	_____
_____	Open Space Technology	60679-605	_____
_____	Appreciative Inquiry	60687-605	_____
_____	The Conference Model	60695-605	_____
_____	Think Like a Genius Process	60709-605	_____
_____	Real Time Strategic Change	60717-605	_____

Shipping and Handling _____
($4.50 for the first packet; $1.50 for each additional packet.)

TOTAL (CA residents add sales tax) $_____

Method of Payment
Orders payable in U.S. dollars. Orders outside U.S. and Canada must be prepaid.

❏ Payment enclosed   ❏ Visa   ❏ MasterCard   ❏ American Express

Card no. _____ Expiration date _____

Signature _____

Name _____ Title _____

Organization _____

Address _____

City/State/Zip _____

Phone (in case we have questions about your order) _____

May we notify you about new Berrett-Koehler products and special offers via e-mail?
E-mail _____

Send Orders to Berrett-Koehler Communications, Inc., P.O. Box 565, Williston, VT 05495 • **Fax** (802) 864-7626 • **Phone** (800) 929-2929
• **Web** www.bkconnection.com